SHORT BLACKS are gems of recent Australian writing – brisk reads that quicken the pulse and stimulate the mind.

SHORT BLACKS

1 Richard Flanagan *The Australian Disease: On the decline of love and the rise of non-freedom*

2 Karen Hitchcock *Fat City*

3 Noel Pearson *The War of the Worlds*

4 Helen Garner *Regions of Thick-Ribbed Ice*

5 John Birmingham *The Brave Ones: East Timor, 1999*

6 Anna Krien *Booze Territory*

7 David Malouf *The One Day*

8 Simon Leys *Prosper: A voyage at sea*

9 Robert Manne *Cypherpunk Revolutionary: On Julian Assange*

10 Les Murray *Killing the Black Dog*

11 Robyn Davidson *No Fixed Address*

12 Galarrwuy Yunupingu *Tradition, Truth and Tomorrow*

THE AUSTRALIAN DISEASE

ON THE *DECLINE* *of* *LOVE* AND THE RISE OF NON-FREEDOM

RICHARD FLANAGAN

SHORT BLACKS

Published by Black Inc.,
an imprint of Schwartz Publishing Pty Ltd
37–39 Langridge Street
Collingwood VIC 3066 Australia
enquiries@blackincbooks.com
www.blackincbooks.com

Originally presented as Liberty Victoria's Alan Missen Oration.
Published in Quarterly Essay 44, *Man-Made World*, Black Inc., 2011.
This edition published 2015.

National Library of Australia Cataloguing-in-Publication entry:
Flanagan, Richard, 1961– author. The Australian disease : on the decline of love and the rise of non-freedom / Richard Flanagan.
9781863957618 (paperback) 9781921870491 (ebook) Short blacks ; no. 1.
Social psychology–Australia. Attitude (Psychology)–Australia. Conformity–Australia. Australia–Politics and government–21st century. Australia–Social conditions–21st century.
306.0994

Cover and text design by Peter Long.

FSC
www.fsc.org
MIX
Paper from responsible sources
FSC® C009448

Printed in Australia by Griffin Press. The paper this book is printed on is certified against the Forest Stewardship Council® Standards. Griffin Press holds FSC chain of custody certification SGS-COC-005088. FSC promotes environmentally responsible, socially beneficial and economically viable management of the world's forests.

RICHARD FLANAGAN's most recent novel *The Narrow Road to the Deep North*, won the 2014 Man Booker Prize.

The Australian Disease was originally presented as Liberty Victoria's Alan Missen Oration, doubling as the Closing Address of the 2011 Melbourne Writers' Festival.

Good evening. I am afraid Richard Flanagan couldn't be here tonight and so I am here in his place. My name is Craig Thomson. You might have heard a lot in recent times about another Craig Thomson. I am not him. I am just a run-of-the-mill bloke who likes prostitutes. A lot. They're great. Really, really great. God I've had some fun. You can do anything if you pay. It's incredible. I even had a Julie Bishop once. She said, You want the stare? I said, You get what you pay for.

Mates say, But how do you afford it? Mate.

I say, you find someone who has your name and a work credit card with a huge limit and you work out where this person is staying and you break into his room. Or just knock. That's what I ended up doing. We got to know each other quite well, and well, he's so busy doing his job, I just borrow his wallet and his phone and ring up and do the ordering.

He never seems to mind, he doesn't really seem to know who I am – it's sort of like a Philip K. Dick novel, doppelgangers and whatever – and then you get down to business. Christ, I was there once, video camera and all, but he didn't seem to notice. He'd be talking to someone important. Like maybe Mark Arbib. Or somebody like that. Perhaps it was another universe or parallel dimension, the ALP, I don't know. All I know is that when I see Craig now he doesn't seem to remember me.

Anyway, Richard Flanagan asked me to read his speech and I'm hoping to borrow his credit card later tonight, so I should begin.

*

How good it is to be here at the end of a marvellous fortnight that has seen literature celebrated in the most wonderful way possible. Whose heart hasn't lifted with joy at all that has taken place in our great city of fiction?

I speak, of course, of Canberra.

In the offices and lobbies and forecourts of Parliament House, the restaurants and bars of Manuka and Kingston, homage has been paid by our leaders to literature in the most sincere way possible, by life seeking to imitate art.

For on this, the fiftieth anniversary of *Catch-22*'s publication, how inspirational it is to see a character clearly modelled on Joseph Heller's Major Major Major Major, forever absent and suddenly somehow supremely present, promoted by bureaucratic error that is the fault of a machine gone haywire – in Major Major Major Major's case an early IBM computer, in Craig Thomson's case a late NSW Labor machine – to centre stage of our nation's public life.

And that, of course, is the catch. Because Craig Thomson shouldn't have been chosen and promoted by the ALP – except that he was and now, of course, he can't be unchosen.

The question arises as to why the ALP endorsed someone like Craig Thomson for the last election, when much of his past would presumably already have been known in ALP circles. And having elevated him, why did the ALP keep promoting him? Why did Craig Thomson get the thumbs up from the Labor Party, why did the Labor Party think this man should be a leader, a lawmaker, a shaper of opinion and of our national future?

And the answer, perhaps, is one that goes to the heart of our present malaise: it is because Craig Thomson was a conformist. And in present-day Australia, it doesn't matter what you do or what you have done, so long as you conform to power. The only true crime in an ever-more bland Australia is to not conform. I don't mean to suggest that conformity is a national characteristic. It is an aspect of the human condition, but only one part. But of late it seems to have become a predominant condition of Australian life. And it is about this Australian disease of conformity that I want to speak tonight, and about how conformity deforms and destroys love and freedom.

Let me begin with a story my father once told me. During the war he was one of "Dunlop's Thousand," that now mythical group of POWs who endured the horrors of the Death Railway under the Japanese, led by a doctor called Weary Dunlop.

One day on the railway a digger called Slappy Oldham turned up to sick parade with a cigarette dangling from the corner of his mouth. An English major called Driscoll made a swipe at Slappy, which the POW evaded by the slightest move of his head.

"Lucky you missed," said Slappy Oldham.

Driscoll angrily demanded to know why.

"If you'd touched me," said Slappy Oldham, "I'd have dropped you, you bastard."

Driscoll grew more agitated and was speaking of charges when Dunlop arrived.

Slappy walked up to him.

"You know that bastard Driscoll?" said Slappy Oldham. "He tried to swipe me, and I told him off."

"Good on you, Slappy," replied Weary, to the amazement of the upper echelon. "Always look after yourself."

I once spent a memorable evening with Dunlop that ended with us drinking in his Toorak mansion, a place where time seemed to have stopped somewhere in the 1930s. I sat on an aged, cracked leather couch and he told me of how as a young doctor in London in the 1930s he had gone into the East End and taken on Oswald Mosley's British Union of Fascists' Blackshirts at their rallies. I knew this was unusual, for Dunlop was a distinguished rugby player, capped for Australia, and Mosley recruited heavily from London rugby circles. So concerned was Dunlop by the rise of fascism, he told me, that he very nearly went to Spain to fight with the International Brigades.

Was he attracted to the Communist Party then? I asked, knowing well how many of the very best at the time had been.

"Not at all," Dunlop said. "I just didn't agree." Dunlop spent his war not agreeing, his methods often involving literature. He said the best way to deal with a Japanese guard was by learning Shakespeare's sonnets. His own weapon of choice when seeking to gain the upper hand in a cat-and-mouse game of asserted authority was Portia's speech from *The Merchant of Venice* on the quality of mercy, which he would declaim in a loud and forceful enough manner to bluff his way out of trouble. Sentenced to death by beheading, he passed what he thought were his final hours reciting Keats' "Ode to a Nightingale."

The central idea of Keats' most famous poem is that the singer may die, but the song is eternal. Dunlop's choices were ever apt.

In his old age the poem that meant most to him was Tennyson's "Ulysses," a poem of an aged king reflecting on what has come to him.

"I am become a name," thinks Ulysses. And so too, Weary Dunlop.

A letter he wrote my father ends with the final stanza of "Ulysses," in which the aged king implores his old colleagues – "free hearts," as he calls them – to follow him back to sea, to

. . . sail beyond the sunset,
and the baths
Of all the western stars until I die. . . .
Tho' much is taken,
much abides; and tho'

We are not now that strength
which in old days
Moved earth and heaven;
that which we are, we are;
One equal temper of heroic hearts,
Made weak by time and fate,
but strong in will
To strive, to seek, to find,
and not to yield.

The poem, particularly this final stanza, is an idea of freedom, of resistance at once utterly futile and somehow entirely necessary, and that idea is in literature closely related to the idea of love. *Catch-22*, a novel of heroic resistance in which the hero recognises he is jeopardising his traditional rights of freedom and independence by daring to exercise them by taking part in a war, begins, like so many novels, with love, Heller's opening sentence reading, "It was love at first sight." In the next paragraph we discover Yossarian has fallen in love with the chaplain.

Love, humour, freedom. From the first great recognisably modern novel, Don Quixote, these three are never very far apart. Do we trust humour because it is the justice the law never is? Do we trust the idea of love, no matter how mad – from Don Quixote's love for the farm girl he renames Dulcinea del Toboso to Yossarian's love for the chaplain – because in the face of conformity, the madder the love, in some mysterious way the greater the commitment to freedom?

"Freedom, Sancho," Don Quixote says, "is one of the most precious gifts bestowed by heaven on man; no treasures that the earth contains and the seas conceal can compare to it; for freedom, as for honour, men can and should risk their lives and, in contrast, captivity is the worst evil that can befall them."

Freedom and love. Both are complex and irreducible and ambiguous. Or, to put it more simply, both are deeply human. And correspondingly, their denial is an attack on what we most value about ourselves. Yet to discover their essence, to live these things, is the mystery with which literature is so often obsessed.

"For one human being to love another," wrote the poet Rainer Maria Rilke, "that is perhaps the most difficult of all our tasks, the ultimate, the last test and proof, the work for which all other work is but preparation."

Few writers of the last hundred years have more bravely attempted to describe the growing difficulty of that task of love than the Soviet writer Vasily Grossman in his last two great novels, *Life and Fate* and *Everything*

Flows, in which Grossman seemed to conclude that politics was the enemy of love.

By 1962, Grossman was dying of stomach cancer. Once one of the most celebrated Russian war journalists and an acclaimed social-realist novelist, Grossman was now in disgrace. The KGB had confiscated all known manuscripts of Grossman's new epic novel of World War II, *Life and Fate*. Grossman met with Mikhail Suslov, chief ideologue of the USSR's Politburo, to beg that his book be published.

Grossman was told that his novel was more damaging to the USSR than Pasternak's recent cause célèbre, *Dr Zhivago*. It could not be published, said Suslov, for 200 years.

Unknown to either Grossman or the KGB, one of Grossman's friends had made a secret copy. Nearly twenty years after

Grossman's death, it was smuggled out of the USSR. Though it made little impact on publication in Switzerland in 1980, it has in the decades since come to be hailed as a twentieth-century *War and Peace*, and with this changing fortune Grossman has secured a reputation as a latter-day Tolstoy.

All praise is a form of incomprehension, and Grossman is a writer more difficult than most to divine. Unlike the great Soviet writers who were products of pre-revolutionary Russia – like Bulgakov and Akhmatova – Grossman was a product of the new order, an insider, a Soviet man.

"Everything I have," he wrote in a letter to the NKVD chief Yezhov in 1938 begging for the release – really, the life – of his arrested wife, "I owe to the Soviet government."

Why this man – a conformist who made his accommodations with the Soviet tyranny, turned his back, averted his eye, held his tongue, signed accusing letters – came to a point where he said "No" to his masters is perhaps unknowable.

Certainly his experience of the war, his witnessing of the Holocaust, the death of his mother at the hands of the *Einsatzgruppen*, Stalin's post-war anti-Semitic campaign, his discovery of love in middle age – a large life, in short, that cannot be detailed here – led Grossman finally to conclude that fascism was simply a mirror response to the "cosmic violence" of Soviet communism. But why this then liberated him to write two masterpieces of the twentieth century remains mysterious.

A few months after his meeting with Suslov, at the height of the Cuban missile crisis on 26 October 1962, the Central Committee heard that Grossman was at work on a new "anti-Soviet" novel. The informer is suspected to have been his stepson, who lived with Grossman.

As the world teetered on the brink of the abyss, this novel was discussed at the highest levels of Soviet leadership. Is it possible to imagine any book today eliciting such fear, bequeathed such strange honour?

The novel was *Everything Flows*, unfinished at the time of Grossman's death in 1964. It was perhaps unfinishable. How strange it is though that somewhere in that abyss between ambition and failure sometimes lies greatness. When first published in English in 1972, *Everything Flows* failed to garner anything like the attention in the West that Solzhenitsyn's work had received. Grossman's idea of history was heretical to almost all. He didn't compare or rank the horrors of the gulag and collectivisation and the Holocaust. Rather, and most chillingly, he connected them.

His anti-politics, of a type that anticipated the great revolts of the 1980s, rendered his work unfathomable for many. The book offered succour neither to the left, for by reviling Lenin and Leninism it broke the ultimate taboo; nor to the right, by offering a damning critique of pre-revolutionary Russia.

His humanism, placing kindness and goodness, truth and freedom, at the centre of life, as both the meaning and fullest expression of life, seemed weak, even quaint, in the face of the cocaine rush of turbo-capitalism that had begun to take all before it in the final decades of the twentieth century with its material wonders and ideological triumph.

In recent years, particularly since the

global financial crisis, Grossman's *Everything Flows* has become the subject of worldwide interest and praise. What has changed is not Grossman, but us. Suddenly, this story seems not about another world many years ago, but speaks to our world now and tomorrow.

The novel is ostensibly simple and could hardly be simpler. In 1957, after thirty years in the gulag, a man returns to a humble life in Russian society. Within it, though, is a book constantly breaking boundaries, flooding over, travelling far from the strange anti-socialist realist, social-realist *Life and Fate*; pointing to the great philosophical novels of Kundera; constantly keeping faith with the idea of story as the vehicle of truth.

The book contains multitudes, and not only of people. Its moods range from the near mystical, in its depiction of women, particularly mothers, to hard political, in its study of Lenin, to epic and elegiac. Grossman somehow penetrates the essence of the USSR in a way few ever did – alive to the psychology and the humanity of its revolutionaries, cannibals, *zeks*, commissars and secret policemen. His stark descriptions of the horrors of the Ukraine famine make one shudder today; I suspect they will have the same effect in centuries to come.

"All the living are guilty," he writes, a judgment he did not exclude himself from. He had signed the letters, he had refused to help, and he bore especial guilt about his mother, whom he felt he should have saved.

The dying Grossman is a novelist now going for broke. Like the dying Bulgakov writing *The Master and Margarita*, he was liberated from fame, success, even the possibility of publication, to be able finally to write what he meant.

Near its end *Everything Flows* breaks its banks again and again: chapters grow shorter, more concentrated, reducing history, thought, human nature, to a dazzling and dizzying poetry.

Grossman makes a chilling historical argument replete with the ultimate Soviet blasphemy, the essence of which is still shocking to come to terms with. That it was written half a century ago makes it even more extraordinary. Grossman argues that the nineteenth-century prophets of the unique Russian soul, from Gogol to Dostoevsky, believed that this soul, once fully realised, would lead the world to a profound spiritual evolution. Their fatal error, according to Grossman, was that they "all failed to see that this soul had been enslaved for a thousand years."

For Grossman, Russian history was that

of a thousand years of slavery. He traces the growing enslavement of the Russian people through the Middle Ages and argues that the progressive achievements of Peter the Great and Catherine the Great were linked to a corresponding increase in what he calls "non-freedom."

In Russia Grossman sees progress and the growth of slavery as inextricably linked, while in the West it is progress and the growth of freedom. And here is the heart of Grossman's terrifying vision: the true consequence of Lenin's revolution was to take this uniquely Russian slavery to the world. This for Grossman is the Russian spectacle that enchants the world: "of modernisation through non-freedom."

For Grossman, Stalin is but a consequence, and an inevitable one at that, of Lenin. And not just Stalin, but fascism. Writing this in the early 1960s in Russia was more than merely blasphemous. It was an historical insight of extraordinary perceptiveness.

"Did Russia's prophets ever imagine," Grossman wrote in the final months of his life, "that their prophecies about the coming universal triumph of the Russian soul would find their grating fulfilment in the unity of the barbed wire stretched around Auschwitz and the labour camps of Siberia?"

Grossman's hero, Ivan Grigoryevich, senses the spirit of the gulag all around him. "Barbed wire, it seemed, was no longer necessary; life outside the barbed wire had become in its essence no different from that of the barracks."

This terrified me when I first read it; that an idea had escaped the gulag and might take the world. I am still shaken by it.

The great irony, according to Grossman,

was that Lenin, through his violence and terror, destroyed not just any possibility of liberation from "the satanic force of Russia's serf past," but hugely advanced its domain. And so, writes Grossman, "Through the will, passion and genius of Lenin, Russia's thousand-year law of development became a worldwide law."

And who looking at China can read this without trembling? Who can contemplate the USA's present stumblings and the rise of the Tea Party movement without wondering? Was the outcome of the Cold War defeat and victory, or was it a strange merging of the worst of two polarities to form our brave new world? The left believes freedom will bring economic progress, the right that economic progress will bring freedom. But what if both are wrong, if Grossman is right, and there is no necessary connection?

"A Putin–Palin ticket," recently suggested Gary Shteyngart – another Russian-Jewish writer whose satires focus on turbo-capitalism's similarities to old-style totalitarianism – "can really cement the liberties Russia has achieved over the last 200 years."

Yet as he journeys through hell, somehow Grossman divines meaning in all this, and is finally hopeful. He concludes that freedom can never be destroyed. For Grossman this is "a sacred law of life: human freedom stands above everything. There is no end in this world for the sake of which it is permissible to sacrifice human freedom."

Half a century after his death it is Grossman's twin insight – his assertion of freedom over politics coupled to his fear of an idea escaping the gulag and taking over the world, this terrifying vision of material progress achieved through non-freedom – that resonates. For we assume freedom when perhaps we are not entirely correct to do so.

Non-freedom to the Western mind is inevitably linked with images of backwardness – Soviet tractors, East German Trabants, Kim Jong Il's haircut. But non-freedom these days is also iPads, iPhones and a dazzling array of less iconic but ubiquitous consumer goods that flood our stores, our homes and which increasingly are used to define our ideas of worth and happiness. It is a full-lipped smile achieved with the aid of collagen made from skin flensed from dead Chinese convicts.

And over the last two decades the idea that escaped the gulag has begun appearing in other more direct ways in Australia. And strangely, there is a growing tolerance of and even active support for these manifestations of non-freedom.

Take, for example, the anti-terrorism laws passed several years ago. Supported by both parties but much and rightly condemned for their draconian and utterly unnecessary provisions for secret trials and secret imprisonment, these laws are profoundly dangerous. As long as they remain on the books an unscrupulous government in difficult circumstances could visit great evil on Australian people. They need reform as a matter of the greatest urgency and yet there is no likelihood they will be reformed.

In the Dr Haneef case we were presented with the disturbing spectre of an innocent man appearing to be framed and imprisoned for what can only be seen as political advantage, in which our security forces would seem to have lied to the Australian public. In 2007 a Sydney court found that an Australian citizen, Izhar Ul-Haque, had been illegally kidnapped and threatened by ASIO operatives. This blatant abuse of power by our secret police and what it might bode for our future seemed of little concern to either major party or the media, and the lack of attention the case received was all the more remarkable given it was held in the middle of the federal election campaign.

A second example is the shameful decision by the federal government, days after it recorded its worst polling on record, to seek to seize David Hicks' earnings from his memoirs. While Chopper Read can boast of feeding people into cement mixers on national television and derive income from his highly successful books, it seems strange in the extreme that a figure whose criminality is a matter of national debate rather than established fact would be pursued by the government in this matter.

It is very hard to escape the suspicion that, having lost a large section of the voting public with its carbon tax, the government sought a few weeks later to win it back with a right-wing play. Why otherwise would the government wait for nine months after a publication that the federal police tracked every step of the way?

David Hicks' supporters contend that Hicks was effectively a political prisoner at Guantanamo. If they are right, then rather than the government seeking to perpetuate the impression Hicks is a criminal by taking money he has earned from his memoirs, the government itself deserves public investigation as to the extent to which it was complicit in allowing Hicks to be tortured and imprisoned because of politics. And for any such investigation to have validity, Hicks' own testimony needs to be widely published and discussed.

If Hicks' supporters are wrong, this deserves to be established, with both sides of the argument being made thoroughly by all involved, not least and most particularly by Hicks himself. Hicks' story was a central one for Australia in recent years and the issues raised are profound for any country that perceives itself as democratic. They therefore deserve the widest and deepest consideration. To seek to seize the profits from his book does not promote that consideration but rather seeks to stifle it.

As the conservative commentator Chris Berg noted, the argument that confiscating David Hicks' commercial gains has nothing to do with free speech is misleading.

"That this argument has come from many conservatives is disappointing," writes Berg, who goes on to argue: "Speech requires finance. To pretend the former is unharmed if you ban the latter is nonsensical. If a government was to ban a newspaper from making a profit but otherwise leave its material uncensored we would not hesitate to condemn it as a violation of freedom of expression."[1]

While the federal government's decision then seems explicable only in terms of the pathetic calculus that is contemporary Australian politics, it creates worrying precedents about the possibilities of future political censorship through the impoundment of income. The inescapable lesson of history is that any power given to the state – even when well meaning in intent – will ultimately be abused by the state. Like freedom, non-freedom does not arrive ready-made. It grows, and no soil should ever be made ready for its sowing.

A third area of growing non-freedom is

our treatment of boat people. If fifty Australians drowned in Sydney Harbour, it would be a national tragedy. But when upwards of fifty refugees drown off the Australian coast, as they did at Christmas Island late last year, it is a political question. Even worse than the varied Pacific laagers proposed by successive governments is the laager of the mind in which both major parties are now incarcerated. Sadly, a Nauru of mentality is immune to judicial review. The racial and social panic that was whipped up to win an election in 2001 has now taken hold to such an extent that neither party can seem to conceive how to approach the matter without resorting to more hysteria.

If Australia does not have a refugee problem like, say, Italy, with over 48,000 refugees arriving since January, it does have a dismal public life largely bereft of courage or humanity, and it has created a national myth that now poisons all sides of politics. The myth is that hordes of refugees will overrun Australia unless harsh policies of dissuasion and internment are employed.

For more than a decade this myth, the issue of opportunism and electoral cynicism, has been a weeping sore at the heart of our public life. It cannot be blamed solely on John Howard's Liberal government. It was the product of a deep cynicism in both major parties and has since become deeply entrenched in no small part because – despite some honourable exceptions – of the lack of courage within either major party to stand up against it.

The strange drift begun in the 1990s under Paul Keating with detention centres and mandatory detention centres was immensely strengthened under John Howard's government. As loony as Hitler's *Lebensraum* in reverse, John Howard's rhetoric of "border protection" struck a similarly popular note. The Labor Party, as noted by US embassy officials in a WikiLeaks cable published the same day as last year's Christmas Island tragedy, was profoundly traumatised by its 2001 election loss and remains haunted by it to the present day. Labor's leadership capitulated to Howard's vision and went largely in lock step with his policies, and on coming to power Julia Gillard has essentially reworked Howard-era policies with a sometimes ludicrous edge.

Wicked as it was, the myth grew only more powerful as the rate of suicide, of self-harm, of simple and utterly unnecessary waste and wreckage of human life among the refugees ballooned. And perhaps even more damaging was the harm we did ourselves.

Numerous psychological studies have demonstrated how human beings can be desensitised to the sufferings of others, how empathy can be eroded to the point where otherwise reasonable people can inflict great suffering in good conscience. Australia over the last two decades has been one vast psychological study in which our leaders have desensitised a nation to the plight of others. There is no good in this, and the portents of where it is leading us in the form of the rise of racist attacks and hate websites, and the growing influence of a new far right, are disturbing.

What does it say of a nation, what does it say to a nation, when in a time of austerity, of slashing of public services, a billion dollars of Australian taxpayers' money is being spent annually to persecute, damage and sometimes destroy the lives of people of whom between 80 and 95 per cent are finally proven to be genuine refugees – that is, to hurt the most powerless and helpless and deserving of help and kindness? It shames us as a nation that claims to be both humane and generous, it belittles us as a people, and none of it will deter the wretched of the earth, forced to choose between despair and hope, from continuing to choose hope.

On 1 September 2011, the prime minister, Julia Gillard, looking and sounding like a dying metronome, criticised the High Court decision that halted the incompetently conceived and ineptly named Malaysian Solution. Admitting that there was now doubt over whether offshore processing was any longer legally possible, she went on to say of refugee law that "The High Court's decision basically turns on its head the understanding of the law in this country."

It would, though, be too much to hope

she's right, to hope it is the beginning of the end of this poisonous and cruel fiction that has for far too long caused so much misery for so little reason, because the one bizarre certainty is that both parties will only harden their rhetoric and redouble their attempts to find a way to ignore or overturn the High Court's decision.

For much of the latter part of the twentieth century Australia seemed to be opening up to something large and good. It believed itself a generous country, the land where battlers got a "fair go." Whatever happened to a fair go? Whatever happened to the battler? Because if an Afghan Hazara isn't a battler, I don't know who is. In the video footage of last year's tragedy it is possible to look down the cliffs of Christmas Island and in the spindrift blown up from below to hear not only the screams of women and children, to see not only the drowned and the drowning and a broken boat, but also to glimpse the promise of what Australia had once been. And with each wave that rolls in, it breaks apart a little more.

And watching this, it is too easy to deride Howard, to dismiss Gillard, to mock Abbott. Far harder to understand the larger drift of our times that has led our politicians to behave so abysmally, to recognise that neither our problems nor their solutions come with party tags. For we have reached a moment in history where politics seems suddenly unequal to the terrible problems that beset us.

If we look at Australia over the last decade and a half, we are presented with the unedifying, indeed disturbing, image of a society whose major institutions failed. This was not necessarily so in other countries. If it is the case, for example, that the past US administration committed crimes – at Abu Ghraib, at Guantanamo, in rendition centres – then it was US journalists who first brought them to public light, it was US legal systems and US lawyers that began bringing them into question, it was US public figures who began pressing for change. Nothing similar happened in Australia.

If we look to another example, that of Britain, we see that it had what we didn't: a major debate in parliament about whether they should go to war in Iraq. On the tombstone of the former British foreign affairs minister, Robin Cook, who resigned his parliamentary positions over the Iraq invasion, are his own poignant words: "I may not have succeeded in halting the war, but I did secure the right of parliament to decide on war." One after another, loyal Tory MPs and loyal Labour

MPs stood up and said they disagreed with their party leadership's support of the war.

To the shame of all Australian parliamentarians, not one here could claim the same epitaph as Cook, for in contrast our parliament was quiescent. In Australia such a questioning of the party leadership's position on any issue has become not just unacceptable, but pilloried in the impoverished judgment of the Canberra press gallery as political suicide. To speak out is to be declared a rat, a party renegade and a political naif. To not speak out is to be rewarded with endorsement and promotion. It is to be Craig Thomson. It is the Australian disease.

And so our parties failed us. Our parliament failed us. Our media failed us. Why they did is difficult to answer, though the answer is clearly to be found in an examination of the new conformity at the heart of Australian life.

What we have witnessed is a corrosion of the idea of the truth and a sustained attack on those whose views differ from that of power. What we have experienced is a coarsening of public rhetoric by standover men who claim to speak for the ordinary Australian, but seem rather to represent only the interests of government and corporate power. They are the belligerati who are given opinion columns and radio talkback programs; who are accorded the status of minor celebrities; and there can at times seem no end to the uniquely Australian cross of their public bullying in defence of private interest at popular expense.

When the Velvet Revolution took place, Václav Havel said the West was wrong to dismiss the experience of Eastern Europe as history. Rather, he said, it was a distorted mirror to what the West could become if it wasn't vigilant.

What we hear parroted in Australia today at ever-shriller frequencies are the old mantras of Stalinism, once used to justify the great crimes of a century, now ironically recycled by the right to defend the indefensible. Those who speak out are inevitably demonised as out-of-touch elites. This pejorative use of the word elite begins with Stalin in 1948, when he used it to describe Jewish intellectuals upon whom he was about to turn his terror.

We are being told, as the old USSR was told, that there are things that matter more than the truth and individual freedom – national security, the needs of the security forces, special international commercial undertakings. But as Vasily Grossman came to conclude, there is nothing higher in this life than the truth and individual freedom. The striving for these two things is the essence of who and what we are.

One of the most potent expressions of our new age is the arrival of a new class, both political player and truth controller, composed of those individuals for whom the role of politician, journalist, minder and senior bureaucrat are just avatars they inhabit, interchangeable ways of exercising power against truth and against freedom.

The phone-hacking scandal, with its revelations of revolving Rubik's cubes of power involving media, politics and police, was an illuminating insight into this new class, which resembles nothing so much as the old class of apparatchik in the Soviet Union, mediocre vessels empty save for vaulting ambition and endlessly craven souls. It's not just that Rupert Murdoch seems to be morphing into Yuri Andropov in a leisure suit. Conformists par excellence, capable only of agreeing with power however or wherever it manifests itself, they are the ones least capable of dealing with the many new challenges we face, precisely because those challenges demand the very qualities the new class lacks: courage, independence of thought and a belief in something larger than its own future.

The new class, understanding only self-interest, believing only in the possibilities of its own cynicism, committed to nothing more than its own perpetuation, seeks to ride the tiger by agreeing with all the tiger's desires, believing it and not the tiger will endure, until the tiger decides it's time to feed, as the mining corporations did with Kevin Rudd, as News Limited is now with Julia Gillard.

Nor does the new class have any answer other than accommodation to the rise of a new far right unseen in the West since the

1930s, a strange and inchoate rage waiting for final and terrible political expression. At a moment in history when the old verities are crumbling, this new far right trades in anger and fear, in conspiracies and known enemies. It promotes a new consensus that celebrates superstition as knowledge, that is hostile to social and racial difference, and celebrates hatred at the expense of reason. It leads to scientists being not just derided, but routinely threatened with death, and intellectual and artistic life seen as at best unnecessary and at worst dangerous. And all because this new rabid right is interested not in truth, but promoting ignorance; not in freedom of all, but the righteous punishment of those it regards as the damned. Rather than recognising the complex task of building lives together in a world of difference, its rhetoric promises an apocalyptic liberation.

Under the rule of the new class, we remain smug and complacent. We ignore the worst global economic crisis since the 1930s as the folly of far lands. We understand a once-in-a-century resource rush as an immortal fact of our own country. We confuse robbing the wealth of our land with an idea of national genius. We mistake corporate success for personal prosperity. Yet a few days after BHP announced a record profit of $22.5 billion, Australia's biggest ever, ABS statistics were released that show Australians' total disposable income fell for the first time in fourteen years. Our gilded recession may well at a certain point become a fullblown recession. Or worse.

Are we ready for what we must deal with? Do we have the political will, the collective empathy, to deal with the social stresses that will inevitably arise without resort to more attacks on our liberties?

We in Australia should not make the error of thinking that the causes of the horrors besetting other countries are unique to them. The hatred and fear of Muslims that motivated Anders Breivik to massacre seventy-six Norwegians is a hatred and fear that is prospering in Australia. The attempted assassination of a US senator earlier this year is an idea of change being given legitimacy by the careless language of both politicians and some sections of the media here in recent months.

We need to remind ourselves that material progress, corporate profits and a mining boom do not need freedom to happen. We should not forget that when BHP was heading towards the seventh-biggest profit in the world's history it did not hesitate to destabilise our elected prime minister for proposing to use a fraction of that profit for the national good.

Democracy suffers most when it is wrongly presumed that its guarantees are to be found in the state or government or party, in history or myths of national goodness. Democracy may be the best antithesis to tyranny, but it is not necessarily wise or good. It can at times be an obscene spectacle guilty of great and historic crimes, that on occasion slaughters its own and others for no good reason, colluding with corporations and corrupting its own. It is often stupid, frequently wrong and not given to great leaps. It is in all this intensely human.

But democracy allows for power and non-freedom to be held in check, and for lies to be undone, and it is sustained in this by the courage of dissent and the wisdom of heresy. It is in the preservation and extension of the liberties of the people that the guarantee of the strengths and worth of democracy is to be found.

Democracy at its best is the ongoing movement of humanity towards a better world. And we see all around us that movement stalling. We see our politics broken, unresponsive to the great questions of the age, unable to name, far less address, the central challenges. It as if this great river has suddenly been halted in its path to the sea of hope.

We need to look the disease of Australia in the eye, the disease of conformity that is ill preparing us for the future. Does Australia still have the courage and largeness it once had when it pioneered the secret ballot and universal suffrage? Or will it simply become the United Arab Emirates of the West, content to roll on for a decade or two more, glossing over its fundamental problems while brown coal and fracked gas keep the country afloat? Does Australia have the desire to move into the twenty-first century, or will it continue its retreat into a past as a colonial quarry for the empires of others, its public life ever more run at the behest of large corporations, its people ever more fearful of others, its capacity for freedom and truth with each year a little more diminished?

"In reading the gospels," wrote Oscar Wilde when in Reading Gaol – and let us not forget that while there he was allowed nothing else to read – "I see the continual assertion of the imagination as the basis of all spiritual and material life, I see also that to Christ imagination was simply a form of love."

One does not have to be a Christian for this to seem a beautiful, and a very true, observation.

Yet in recent times we seem to have lived through not so much a crisis of politics as a collapse of that most human attribute, empathy, a collapse so catastrophic it sometimes appears to be a crisis of love, manifest in epidemics of loneliness and depression. It is a crisis most evident in the strange echoing cyber-caverns of the internet, where a convict in a Chinese gulag, physically exhausted, regularly beaten, may after twelve-hour days labouring in a coal mine be forced to play World of Warcraft online in a practice known as gold farming. To earn online credits for his prison bosses to trade for cash, he may find himself pitted against a far right-wing Norwegian extremist who is planning a massacre to save his idea of the world from another idea of the world that only exists online and in his mind. There is contact here, even communion. But does this world create empathy, or destroy it?

In recent years I have come to recognise the wisdom of Vasily Grossman's final novels. Perhaps our homeland is simply the people we love and who love us. Perhaps the only party of honour is the party of one. Perhaps the world advances to a better place through the countless acts of everyday goodness shown by millions of people too easily dismissed as everyday. None of this amounts to an answer to any of our problems, I know. But as Rilke said, "Live the questions." Questions lead to poetry, science, freedom. Certainties lead to Andrew Bolt's blog.

We need politics like we need sewerage, and like sewerage we should want it to work properly and well but not make too much of it, not create of it a fetish by glorifying it with daily celebrations and watching it incessantly on 24-hour TV stations. We in Australia make too much of our political leaders and their work, their failings, their strivings, their successes, and too little of ourselves. For if we take our compass from power we will inevitably arrive at despair, whereas if we take our compass from those around us we will arrive at hope.

There are so many forces in the world that divide us deeply and murderously. We cannot escape politics, history, religion, nationalism – for their sources lie as deep in our hearts as love and goodness, perhaps even deeper. In a world where the road to the new tyrannies is paved with the fear of others, we need to rediscover that we are neither alone, nor in the end that different, that what joins us is always more important than what divides us, and that the price of division is ever the obscenity of oppression.

We need once more to assert the necessity of witnessing and questioning as the greatest guarantee we can have of freedom. If I am left believing in anything, it is something very simple: that truth matters above all else. Anything that honours and guarantees the truth is not just good, but necessary. And anything, like mass conformity, that threatens the truth needs to be challenged. For the road to tyranny is never opened with a sudden coup d'état. It is a long path paved with the small cobbles of silence, lies and deceit that ends, inevitably and terribly, in horror.

In the end none of these things is ever a matter of party. Weary Dunlop most likely voted Liberal, yet it is no paradox that Tom Uren, once known as the heart of the left, said he learnt his socialism from Weary Dunlop while a POW. Tom Uren, like Weary Dunlop, didn't agree. And while a Labor man through and through, Uren has described the Greens' Bob Brown, another man who doesn't agree, as having the blood of Mandela flowing in his veins. These are matters of character and, to use a word little heard these days, courage. More than ever, in this new age, Australians need once more to recover their voice, and that power of not agreeing with power. It's time, like Slappy Oldham, we looked after ourselves a little more, and deferred to power and its Driscolls a little less.

Like the aged Weary Dunlop we could do worse than ponder Ulysses' exhortation to freedom:

> *To follow knowledge*
> *like a sinking star,*
> *Beyond the utmost bound*
> *of human thought.*

Perhaps freedom is finally a form of love. It is unachievable, elusive, Rilke's hardest test that we are destined repeatedly to fail, the greatest challenge, the pursuit of which takes us through an endless cycle of trials and ordeals. But it is our Ithaka, and in our journeying towards it there can be no cease.

4 SEPTEMBER 2011

ENDNOTES

1 Chris Berg, "Free speech: Hicks should keep his memoir profits," *The Drum*, 10 August 2011, www.abc.net.au/unleashed/2831862.html.

SHORT BLACKS

Richard Flanagan's perceptive, hilarious, searing exposé of the conformity that afflicts our public life.

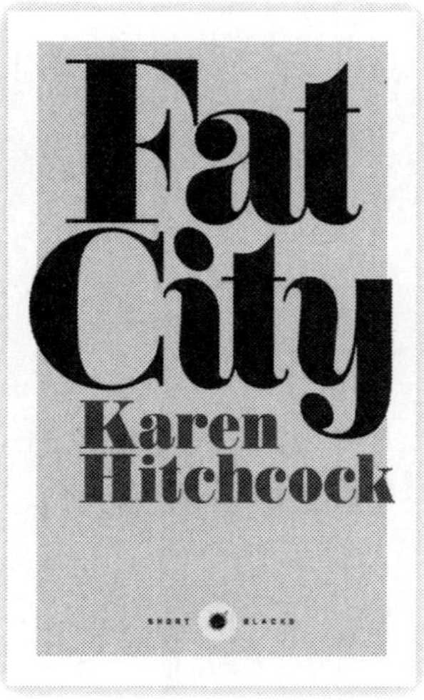

In a riveting blend of story and analysis, doctor and writer Karen Hitchcock explores chemistry, psychology and impulse to excess to explain the West's growing obesity epidemic.

WWW.SHORTBLACKS.COM

CLASSIC SHOTS OF
AUSTRALIAN WRITING

Noel Pearson considers
the most confronting issue
of Australian history:
the question of genocide,
in early Tasmania
and elsewhere.

Helen Garner tells the tale
of a journey to Antarctica
aboard the *Professor*
Molchanov, spanning
icebergs, tourism, time,
photography and the many
forms of desolation.

WWW.SHORTBLACKS.COM

SHORT BLACKS

John Birmingham's unflinching account of the Indonesian Army's Battalion 745 as it withdrew from East Timor after the 1999 independence vote, leaving a trail of devastation in its wake.

Anna Krien takes a clear-eyed look at Indigenous binge-drinking, and never fails to see the human dimension of an intractable problem, shining a light on its deep causes.

WWW.SHORTBLACKS.COM

CLASSIC SHOTS OF AUSTRALIAN WRITING

David Malouf traces the meaning of Anzac Day and shows how what was once history has now passed into legend, and how we have found in Anzac Day 'a truly national occasion.'

Simon Leys' exceptionally beautiful and elegiac essay about a summer spent on the crew of a tuna-fishing boat in Brittany.

WWW.SHORTBLACKS.COM

CLASSIC SHOTS OF AUSTRALIAN WRITING

Robyn Davidson's fascinating and moving essay about nomads explores why, in times of environmental peril, the nomadic way with nature still offers valuable lessons.

Galarrwuy Yunupingu tells of his early life, his dealings with prime minsters, and how he learnt that nothing is ever what it seems.

WWW.SHORTBLACKS.COM